AM NOT ALONE JESUS
IS WITH ME

By Tella Olayeri

All rights reserved under International Copyright Law. Content may not be reproduced in whole or in part or in any form without the consent of the publisher.

Email; tellaolayeri@gmail.com
Website tellaolayeri.com.ng

US Contact
Ruth Jack
14 Milewood Road
Verbank
N.Y.12585
U.S.A. +19176428989

APPRECIATION

I give special appreciation to my wife **MRS NGOZI OLAYERI** for her assistance in ensuring that this book is published and our children that play around us to encourage us day and night.

Also, this manuscript wouldn't have seen the light of the day, if not for the spiritual encouragement I gathered from my father in the Lord, **Dr. D.K. OLUKOYA** who served as spiritual mirror that brightens my hope to explore my calling (Evangelism).

We shall all reap our blessings in heaven but the battle to make heaven is not over, until it is won.

PREFACE

We have a common enemy who seeks to keep and held us in bondage. He is Satan. He is against our freedom and growth. If we are to succeed, we must be aware of his antics and have courage for freedom. If not, it may cause fear and distortion in our life and can affect our whole life. Our past can invade our present and affect our future.

Really life situations can't be smooth all through. Life is not a straight line that would never be fluctuations. In the journey of life, we will encounter obstacles. Sometimes it gets darker, we felt alone, when we are getting nearer. We must believe that the challenges we experience now are temporal. It shall not keep us down, but for us to forge ahead no matter what. At times, these challenges are the creations of the devil to slow down our success, but I assure you, we have reached the turning point and shall succeed.

To be alone is not a good option to life. This day, things are falling apart, the Centre could not hold. Many are left alone; as things are not rosy as before. What shall we say of today's challenging global economy, that form huge increase in the number of independent adult children in the home? It is as if they are left alone not knowing what to do. They form the worst job market of this generation, huge number of graduate adult children that face more economic uncertainty than their parents who were born at a time of relatively greater opportunity and promise. These adult children felt alone and dejected.

Above all, it is not always good at times to be in the crowd; at times you must be alone. To be alone makes you a majority, because you are with God.

Find out more in this book. I say good-luck.

TELLA OLAYERI

PREVIOUS PUBLICATIONS OF THE AUTHOR

1. Fire for Fire Prayer Book Part 1

2. Fire for Fire Prayer Book Part 2

3. Bye Bye to Poverty Part 1

4. Bye Bye to Poverty Part 2

5. My Marriage Shall Not Break

6. Prayer for Pregnant Women

7. Prayer for Fruit of the Womb

8. Children Deliverance

9. Prayer for Youths and Teenagers

10. Magnetic Prayer for Singles

11. Victory over satanic house Part 1

12. Victory over satanic house Part 2

13. I Shall Excel

14. Atomic Prayer Points

15. Goliath at the gate of marriage

16. Deliverance from Spirit of Dogs

17. Naked warriors

18. Power to Overcome Sex in the Dream

19. Strange Women! Leave My Husband Alone

20. *Dangerous Prayer against Strange Women*

21. *Solution to Unemployment*

22. *630 Acidic Prayer Points*

23. *Prayer for Job Seekers*

24. *Power to Retain Job and Excel in Office*

25. *Warfare in the Office*

26. *Power to Overcome Unprofitable Wealth*

27. *Command the Year*

28. *Deliverance Prayer for First Born*

29. *Deliverance Prayer for Good Health and Divine Healing*

30. *Warfare Prayer against Untimely Death.*

31. *Dictionary of Dreams*

32. *Discover Gold and Build Wealth*

33. *My Head is not for Sale*

34. *830 Prophecies for the head*

35. *30 Power Points for the Head*

36. *Prayer after Dreams*

37. *Prayer to Locate Helpers*

38. *Anointing for Eleventh Hour Help*

39. *100% Confessions and Prophecies to Locate Helpers*

40. *Hidden Treasures Exposed!*

41. Prayer to Cancel Bad Dreams

42. Prayer to Remember Dreams

43. 1010 Dreams and interpretations

44. 650 Dreams and Interpretation

45. 1,000 Prayer Points for Children Breakthrough

46. Emergency telephone calls of God

47. I Am Not Alone

48. My Well of Honey shall not dry

49. Shake Heaven with Praises

50. Deliverance prayer for Middle Born Part One

51. 800 Deliverance prayer for Middle Born Part Two

52. Deliverance prayer for Last Born Part One

53. 800 Deliverance prayer for Last Born Part Two

Table of Contents

I AM NOT ALONE 10

WHEN LONELY AND FEARFUL 33

PROPHECY FOR CHAMPIONS 45

CHAPTER ONE

I AM NOT ALONE

"Yet I am not alone because the father is with me" John 16:32

From creation, God didn't want us to be alone. It was a right given to us, but circumstances drew us close to loneliness. When he created Adam, he filled the vacuum by creating Eve. Ever since then, the issue of loneliness was addressed. When God destroyed the earth with flood in the Bible, He silenced spirit of loneliness. Everything He spared was in two(s), male and female. Up till today, whenever we call upon the Lord, He appears. For this reason, we must claim we are not alone even if mother, father, relatives, friends or neighbours desert us. God is with us and shall never desert us. Hence, you can say, "I am not alone".

Do you think you are isolated? Are you dejected thinking you are alone? Do you think God can't stretch his hands far and wide to rescue you without moving from one spot? Our God is all powerful and omnipresent. His hand is not too short to save. He is willing, and ever willing to save and be with us.

God in his perfection sends helpers on board to erode powers of loneliness in our life. When he gives assignment, he readily makes room for helpers. At first, one may view a task as enormous but as you obey or take divine instruction, things become easy. Suddenly, you see people investing in you. When Moses thought he will be alone in Pharaoh's court, God sent him Aaron. Moses influenced Joshua; Elizabeth helped Mary; Jonathan and David were like brothers, Priscilla and Aquila tutored Apollo; Ananias laid hands of deliverance on Paul. Phillip saw the Ethiopian eunuch through. Abraham was there for Lot. When you think you are alone, God shall send a helper.

The fact remains, following Jesus is an adventure complete with struggles and joys. The statement, "I am not alone", is biblical as spelt out in John 16:32. It is a statement of assurance. It is an extension of divine hands of protection from the heavenly.

To say, "I am not alone", connotes believe in the existence of the Almighty, as the All Companion and Protector of life. It means the man of war is with you, ready to extend hands of protection to you and see you through with eyes of safety.

To say, "I am not alone", suggests you are in the path of forward march, backward never; to claim and to possess your possession. You ignore all odds in your way to breakthrough, and challenge barricades and obstacles that may stir at you.

To say, "I am not alone", mean you are unshakeable. You believe in the word and claim the promises there in. You declare yourself as one guided by the Word.
To say, "I am not alone", suggest the saying; 'In the midst of calamity, I shall not be consumed'. The three Hebrews felt this way. They marched in oneness, in the seven times heated furnace of fire unhurt. The fourth man appeared in the fire with them, meaning they are not alone.

To say, "I am not alone", is a breakthrough agenda; meaning that, if others fail to harvest, yours shall be different. What you claim is, the Lord shall see your seed through for great harvest.

To say, "I am not alone" connotes divine favour and anointing for surplus. Favour has magnet of success and prosperity. Favour ushers you to mountain top and announce you for greatness. It announces your arrival wherever you go and makes room for you to be accepted. It separates you for good. This is your dividend when you say, "I am not alone".

To say, "I am not alone" suggests, even if men reject's you, God shall accept and promote you. It means you depend on God for promotion and advancement.

When you say, "I am not alone", it suggests marital fruitfulness. You claim blissful marriage and a home of joy. It suggests, as a bachelor or as a spinster, God shall provide you with the bone of your bone, and the flesh of your flesh.

The agony, sorrow and outcry caused by corruption are enormous this day. Hence the shout of "I am not alone", in every tips. Laughter and joy are rare in the face of people. Today, corruption and threats have stolen the empowerment, opportunity and future of most citizens, which make many to think it, is better to die than to be alone.

The question is, why do corruptions strive so much? It is because we glorify riches which sources are unknown. What then can be done? It is simple. Our society, including our leaders must have a change of mind. We must not worship and be a slave to money. If we don't worship money, I believe redemption shall not be far from us. From here we shall head towards the level of our dreams.

When a country is in dilemma, joy is hardly seen in the faces of citizens. Such country is like a child without parents, a military without its commanding officer or a ship without its captain. All the while, the country is stagnant; not sure of what to do and how to proceed. It is as if the hangs man noose is intact. Terrorists wreak havoc and death at will unchallenged. The country looks helpless as if she is alone.

Situations at times make people believe they are alone. They believe they are isolated and rejected. Even when they claim, "I am not alone, God is with me" in public, right inside them they doubt it. They doubt it because of the negatives that surround them and unkindness of people to them. The fact is, people and government can be unkind to a person at times, but you must not let that make you lose focus. They can be unkind even when you do well. You can be paid evil for good. They can be unkind even without knowing it. They can be unkind at your achievement. They can be unkind and hostile at a person or a community as a result of talents or resources bestowed on them.

The Lord is on our side. In his early sojourn in life, Abraham thought he was alone. When he entered Egypt, he told his wife Sarah to disguise herself as sister, not as his wife. The Bible records it.

"Behold now, I know that thou are a fair woman to look upon: therefore, it shall come to pass, when the Egyptians shall see thee, that they shall say, this is his wife: and they will kill me, but they will save thee alive.

Say, I pray thee, thou art my sister: that it may be well with me for thy sake, and my soul shall live because of thee" *Genesis 12:11-13*.

Abraham had a narrow thought of life. He was afraid, defeated by fear in his heart he instructed his wife to deny she was his wife. He saw soldiers in place, he had not much in him, and worst, he was a stranger. He couldn't understand their language.

But God dramatized his power to Abraham and his wife. He was not only protected but was favoured. As you are reading this book, you may have lost hope concerning a course, thinking all is lost. I pray that the Almighty God shall arise in your situation, to protect and favour you, in the name of Jesus. Amen.

Loneliness can be a matter of rejection. When you are rejected wherever you go, when people refuse to associate with you when you are given a task that abandoned you to a particular place, you are said to be rejected or be alone. When you are denied justice, you are said to be alone.

It is more pathetic when your source of livelihood is denied or when someone who champion the course of liberation is killed or hanged. For example, natives in the creek areas of my country where crude oil is explored believed they were alone. They felt cheated and neglected. It is more pronounced in the delta area of **Ogoni people.** The pollution of the land occasioned by years of exploration and the killing of a man, who championed the cause of injustice against his people, **Ken Saro-Wiwa**, was to them a disaster. Till date, the Ogoni people often recall the brutal execution of the environmental activist and eight other Ogoni sons by the then military government of **General Sanni Abacha** in November 10, 1995.

On the day of the incidence there was loud cry and lamentations across the land as they shouted, "We are left alone; Ken Saro-Wiwa has been killed. Our leaders have been murdered" "Our hope is gone". "We are left alone". What a tragedy that befell the goose that lay the golden egg.

After a long while the hope of Ogoni people became a little bright when the country went for democracy. The situation which attracted interest of Committee of nations prompted the then president to invite the **United Nations Environment Program (U.E.P.)** in the year 2006. The invitation was for U.N.E.P. to assess the extent of pollution in Ogoni land and proffer a far-reaching solution to the devastation.

At last, U.N.E.P. recommended that an urgent clear up to the area be carried out. But to the surprise of Ogoni people not much had been done to neutralize the 'poison' in the land including the contamination of underground with large quantity of a **poisonous substance, Benzene.**

Based on this, they believed that the government of the day turned blind eyes to their predicament. They knew, they were dying gradually as a result of poisoned water and the pollution of their environment. To this, they cried out loud in the manner; "We produce the wealth of the nation, yet we are left alone" I pray this shall not be their portion. The wealth they create shall not consume them. Amen.

The Lord is mighty and awesome. He operates in various windows with multiple functions of signs and wonders, of miracles and perfections. Abraham thought he was alone, but God opened window of fruitfulness for him. When the Israelites left Egypt, they saw the Red Sea in their front and the army of Egypt pursuing them with aggression behind, they thought they were alone. They confronted Moses with anger.

"They said to Moses, "Was it because there were no graves in Egypt that you brought us to the desert to die? What have you done to us by bringing us out of Egypt? 'Leave us alone; let us serve the Egyptians'? It would have been better for us to serve the Egyptians than to die in the desert" Exodus 14:11-12

They thought they were alone, but then the fear that gripped them was silenced by God. The Lord was with them. He parted the Red Sea. They passed through the Red sea unhurt while the Egyptians that did the same were consumed by it. I pray, every stubborn pursuer that refuses to turn back from pursuing you shall perish in the Red sea. Amen.

When the children of Israel were thirsty in the desert, they thought they were alone and forgotten by God. For this, they insulted Moses the more. But God opened rivers of water from the Rock, water gushed out of the Rock! They drank till they were full and filled their empty vessels.

When the children of Israel crave for meat, they became frustrated. They thought they were alone. They confronted Moses, and mere lifting up his eyes to God answer came like a rush. God answered them by sending down manna and quail from heaven. They ate until they were filled. The Bible records it.

"Yet he gave a command to the skies above and opened the doors of the heavens; he rained down manna for the people to eat, he gave them the grain of heaven. Men ate the bread of angels: he sent them all the food they could eat… they ate till they had more than enough" Psalm 78:23-29.

The children of Israel breathe the breath of life after eating more than enough. They thought they were alone, only to discover that the Lord Almighty was with them. Is feeding allowance lacking at home? Don't entertain fear or reproach, the Lord Almighty shall not let you down. He that created you and blessed your marriage with children shall not let you down. Windows of heaven shall open for your sake. Amen.

I AM NOT ALONE JESUS IS WITH ME

Elisha was alone before river Jordan, but God opened window of separation for his sake, and the Jordan parted way for Elisha to pass. I pray that every obstacle or barrier on your way shall part way before you. Amen

Elijah was alone in Mount Carmel; he killed the prophets of Baal that contested with him. To the amazement of the Israelites, he won the day. I pray, those who thought you are alone, and want to contest with you; either in the dream or in the physical shall fail and be defeated, in the name of Jesus. Amen.

Naaman was alone at river Jordan where he dipped himself seven times and was cleansed of leprosy. Brethren are you sick or afflicted and people distance themselves from you? Summon courage and believe you are not alone. The Lord is by your side. He shall heal you with the balm of Gilead. He shall open window of healing for your sake and heal you. By his stripes you are healed! Amen.

David was alone as a poor shepherd in the wilderness, but God was with him. Imagine, your lad was left behind in the farm or in a thick forest, when others arrive home, you won't take it lightly. But this young lad was sent daily to go after the family's flock in the desert alone; exposed to danger. Anytime he thought he was alone, Yahweh stood by him.

David was alone in the wilderness as a shepherd of his father's flocks, when bear appeared to attack the sheep he killed it. Not only this, when lion appeared to kill the sheep, he killed it. I pray, any animal that appear to destroy you either in the dream or in the physical shall die in the name of Jesus. Amen.

David was alone with the boasting Goliath in the battle field. He killed him with the first shot of stone with the sling he held. Whenever David was alone, supernatural forces were by him, to protect and make hero out of him. I pray, the Lord Almighty shall stand by you and make hero out of you. Amen.

Today, many people thought they were alone, but God is with them. They thought they are orphans, but God is with them. Some thought as widow, they are alone, but God is saying "I am with you, fear not, I am your husband" Some are jobless, thinking they are alone, but God is by their side. Some are in court, thinking all is lost, yet they are not alone, God shall bring glory on their side.

"When the Lord brought back the captives to Zion, we were like men who dreamed" Psalm 126:1. I pray, what you lost till this day, God shall return them one hundred fold in the name of Jesus. Amen

There are men and women who felt they are alone. They experience trials, sorrow and rejection. They felt bad and uncomforted. Friends and relatives flee as if a plague. But then something strange happens in their life. Such time make them think deep. They learn lessons and ways to adjust. They turn out to be someone loaded with ideas and knowledge. Their wisdom surpasses those walking the street. When people go to them for counsel, they speak right words and give the very counsel they are longing for. They are loved by men, but then we don't realize the cost which they paid to become so skillful in binding up the gaping wounds and drying tears.

Are you moved by this? Yes of course. But then, if you investigate their past history, you would find that they have suffered more than most. They have stood by ebbing tides and noon sets all alone, but these has been, to make them nurses, the physicians, the priest of men.

The fact is, the boxes that come from foreign climes are rough enough, but they contain spices which scent the air with the fragrance of the Orient. Suffering is rough and hard to bear; but it hides beneath it disciple, education, possibilities which not only leave us bolder, but perfect us to help others.

From the study of life, there is no time you are alone, but with the Father. There is a plus in you all the time. Steel is iron plus fire; soil is rock plus heat, or glacier crushing, linen is flax plus the bath that cleanse. You must have a plus attach to yourself. Hence, you can see that, you can never be alone.

It is good to resign faith to God, whenever you think you are alone. It is with faith Abraham walked with God. When he was instructed by God to leave his father's house to a land of promise, he felt in his mind, in as much he heard the voice, though he saw no one giving the command; he believed he was not alone. With faith he left and sojourn to a land he knew not!

With faith, you march ahead without fear. Even in the jungle faith is needed, in the valley faith is needed as well; in the valley of the shadow of death faith is a must to have. At all times faith is needed as weapon for accomplishment. There is always a large balance to our credit in the bank of heaven waiting for our exercise of faith in drawing it. Draw heavily upon His resources. Faith will bring heaven to your soul.

In the midst of hustle and bustle of life, we do a great deal of good to ourselves if we get used to staying alone with God in prayers, and this is God's clarion call to all and sundry today. A man who knew how to be alone, build a nation by it. His name was Jacob, who became Israel as a result of praying to God alone. He left his family and everything he had and stayed alone with God in prayer.

"That night Jacob got up and took his two wives, his two maid servants and his eleven sons and crossed the ford of the Jabbok. After he had sent them across the stream, he sent over all his possessions. So <u>Jacob was left alone,</u> and a man wrestled with him till day break" Genesis 32:22-24.

The prophet Hosea later bore eloquent tribute to the heroics of Jacob at the altar of prayer, when he said,
"He struggled with the angel and overcome him, and he wept and begged for his favour. He found him at Bethel and talked with him there" Hosea 12:4.

This is what happens at the altar of prayer, when you think you are alone. You become stronger on your knees and prevail. You bring down hands of God in your situation, and silence powers assign against you.

It is high time we explore spiritual march to achieve results. The Lord gave command to the Israelites,
"Every place that he sole of your foot shall tread upon, that have I given unto you" Joshua 1:3. The

children of Israel are to commence march of the Promised Land if they are to take all. Unfortunately, they never did that to more than one-third of the property, and consequently they never had more than one-third, they had just what they measured off, and no more.

When you want to march and possess, do it with all strength in you. Marching and quick marching are much easier to God's warriors than standing still, the Israelites march on out of Egypt, through the desert and won.

The Apostles marched on and converted souls to Christ. Paul was a Field Marshal in the marching order. He preached to the gentiles and was noted for it. Aaron marched and met Moses coming from the wilderness before the palace warfare took place. Elijah marched on for forty days without food in the wilderness. Saul marched on before he could discover Samuel the prophet who anointed him king over Israel to his surprise. The fact remains you cannot be on a spot and win. You must march and have attitude of marching on.

Today, many are chained in the spirit, but walk about in the physical. They can't succeed in real life, because they shall soon fail and fall. Many sat in one spot, glued to seat of darkness, they can't excel. There are those in deep sleep when they should be on marching order, they shall wallow in poverty. It is good to march on and possess your possession.

In the midst of warfare be like an infantry soldier. The infantry is always on ground. The infantry is exposed to fury of the enemy, cold, heat, rain, hazards and every form of danger. Infantries fight without looking back. It is the infantry that is decorated with medals and when sun shines, it shines on the medals and he smiles. He becomes a star. When he goes to the garden, he sees a star, and that star is the infantry.

In the garden is the flower. The sun shines on it and bring strength to it. The light looks at the flower and the flower look at the light. There is contact and communion and power pass into the flower. It held up its head, open its petals, its glory shows and seem fairer and better. That flower is you. You are not alone; heavenly touch is in your life.

For our petals to shine, for our stars to rise and shine, for eagle in us to fly high, we must go into violent prayer. In prayer we invite God into our life. We become majority, even when alone because the Lord is with us

Let's go into the act of prayer now, and shout 'I am not alone'!

PRAYER POINTS

1. O Lord, widen the gap between me and loneliness, in the name of Jesus

2. Any arrow fired to terminate my spouse, go back and consume your sender in the name of Jesus

3. Any arrow fired to terminate my children, go back and consume your sender, in the name of Jesus

4. Any arrow fired to terminate me, go back and consume your sender, in the name of Jesus

5. Any arrow fired to terminate my relations, go back and consume your sender, in the name of Jesus

6. O Lord, don't turn your ear against me, listen to my petition and protect me in the name of Jesus

7. O Lord, stretch your hand of love to me, in the name of Jesus

8. My helpers, locate me and help me, in the name of Jesus

9. Every obstacle between me and my helpers, scatter in the name of Jesus

10. Every task around me, receive divine solution, in the name of Jesus

11. Helpers that will invest in me, locate me and do it, in the name of Jesus

12. My life is, 'forward march, backward never' in the name of Jesus

13. When I pass through the valley of the shadow of death, I shall not die, in the name of Jesus

14. When I march through the fire, I shall not be consumed, in the name of Jesus

15. Favour of God, locate me today, in the name of Jesus

16. Any power assign against my promotion and advancement, meet double failure in the name of Jesus

17. Spirit of rejection in my life, die, in the name of Jesus

18. My source of wealth shall not dry in the name of Jesus

19. My helper shall not die before he/she helps me in the name of Jesus

20. I am loaded with signs and wonders of the Lord, in the name of Jesus

21. Stubborn pursuers assign to pursue me, summersault and die, in the name of Jesus

22. Every Red Sea, assign to swallow me, dry up, in the name of Jesus

23. I shall not be thirsty to insult God, in the name of Jesus

24. Every dark judgment passed against me, be nullified in the name of Jesus

25. I overcome trial and sorrow in the name of Jesus

26. O Lord, fill me with heavenly wisdom in the name of Jesus

27. Divine power that add value to life, locate me, in the name of Jesus

28. Every dark chain that bind me to one spot, break, in the name of Jesus

29. My star, arise and shine in the name of Jesus

30. I shall not sit in darkness in the name of Jesus

31. Power to pray and get favour of God, locate me, in the name of Jesus

CHAPTER TWO

WHEN LONELY AND FEARFUL

We have a common enemy who seeks to keep and held us in bondage. He is Satan. He is against our freedom and growth. If we are to succeed, we must be aware of his antics and have courage for freedom. If not, it may cause fear and distortion in our life and can affect our whole life. Our past can invade our present and affect our future.

Loneliness is loaded with short comings. It is as a result of distancing our self from people. Anyone hunted with spirit of loneliness doesn't know what it is like to desire help and to depend on others. Emotions such as anger and fear become attach to past traumatic experiences in him/her. Slowly he/she begin to lose his/her humanity and tenderness and replace them with hardness. The fact remains, the more you isolate yourself from people; the less you know how to relate to people. The less you know how to relate to people, the more you avoid them. It is a vicious circle. You are emotionally cut off from the real world.

Loneliness, can safely be said not a 'spiritual' problem, and may be said not to have 'spiritual' answer. The problem lay deep in emotions. You are imprisoned by your past choices and experience. Your emotions make you lonely and God seems far away, as the moon.

What most people don't know is; God intends us to love and care for each other on the human as well as on the spiritual level. Genuine and deep friendship is normal not sinful attraction for lust.

To be alone at times doesn't mean God is far, he may have design it that way. Many at times when situations made us lonely we believe something is wrong somewhere. Loneliness doesn't mean a cry of emergency. No bird is so solitary as the eagle. Eagles never fly in flocks; one, at most two, ever being seen at once.

Loneliness at times doesn't mean defeat. There is a strange strength conceived in it. In time of emergency seek to be lonely to discover yourself. God may have created it for discovery. Crows go in flocks and wolves in packs, but the lion and the eagle are solitaries. Strength at times requires quietness which can be gained in solitary. The lake must be calm if the heavens are to be reflected on its surface.

Peter was in prison, lonely and awaiting execution. It was a critical situation full of fear. He faced emergency situation that cry for urgent answer. The church has no higher human power or influence to save him. There was no earthly help except heavenly. Peter was there in prison chained, with Iron Gate locked. God sent his angel that eventually set him free. I pray in every situation you call loneliness; the Lord Almighty shall arise and set you free. Amen

Your situation may be critical in this manner, no hope, no connection, no finance, no security. Yet, there may be some Iron Gate in your life that blocked your way. Like a caged bird you have often beaten against the bars. But, I prophesy unto your life, you shall be set free and receive permanent freedom, in the name of Jesus.
God is seeking for eagle-men and women. There is joy to be alone with God, than be in the midst of crowd. To be left alone without God is dangerous; to be left alone with God is a fore taste of heaven. We find **Abraham** alone in Horeb upon the

heights, but Lot, dwelling in Sodom with multitude. **Jacob** was alone with God when he became a prince. He must be left alone if the angel of God is to whisper in his ear the mystic name of Shiloh. The greatest miracle of **Elijah** and **Elisha** took place when they were alone with God. **Daniel** must be left alone if he is to see celestial vision.

John the Baptist was alone in the wilderness proclaiming Christ the King. **Paul**, who was filled with Greek learning and has also sat at the feet of Gamaliel, must go into Arabia and learn the desert life with God. **Cornelius** was alone praying when angel came to him. No one was with **Peter** on the housetop, when he was instructed to go to the Gentiles. **John the beloved** must be banished to Patmos if he is deeply to take and firmly to keep, 'The Spirit of heaven'. God designed it this way, yet they were not alone!

Are you lonely, deserted and fearful? Jesus is ready to come into your life. The demon possessed man in Gadarenes was lonely and lived among the tombs and hills, unattended to. He suffered much in the hands of Satan. When Jesus came to his life, he was set free. He struggled in vain without sympathy from people. Instead, he was dumped and left alone, until he came across Jesus who healed and set him free. I pray, any power that wants to torment you shall fail in the name of Jesus Christ. Amen.

To be alone at times serve as tunnel of strength. Our **Lord Jesus Christ** loved the people but he often goes away from them for a brief season. He tried every little while to withdraw from the crowd; stealing away at evening to the hills.

When you see yourself in lonely situation, don't call it emergency and quit. Let's take Paul as a case study. To him the prison becomes a palace. It was like looking out over the top of his prison wall and over the heads of his enemies. He bent down not minding his circumstance, wrote epistles of hope and deliverance. He wrote it not as a prisoner of Festus, nor of Caesar; not as a victim of the Sanhedrin, but as the "prisoner of the Lord". Instead of building life on hopelessness, he built hope and courage to forge ahead.

To what can we compare the BIG heart of Paul? A man restrained from the missionary work he loved, was caged in prison. There, he built a new pulpit- a new witness stand. From this situation he never bargains for, lonely as ever, come some of the sweetest and most helpful ministries of Christian liberty. Till this day, the world witness precious messages of light from those dark shadows of captivity.

The life of Paul was drenched with so much blood, and blistered with so many tears, yet he summons courage to live on. Paul did not only know the way to victory, but the laws of victory. He knew there is compensation in every sorrow, and the sorrow is working out the compensation. He knew joy sometimes need pain to give it birth. Paul's suffering was a wonderful fertilizer that gave him courage. He faced hedges of all sorts and hindrances in all directions. Those who suffer most are capable of yielding most.

What more? Paul passed through hardships; he paid the price and won the race. No wonder it is said, hardship is the price of coronation. Paul knew where he was going even before death. In his statement, ***"I have fought a good fight. I have won the race"*** The hardships you endure today are given by the Master for the purpose to win your crown.

Does such bondage – loneliness end with Paul? No, for twelve long years **Bunyan's** lips were silenced in **Bedford jail.** It was there he did the greatest and best work of his life. There he wrote the book that has been read next to the Bible.

Can we speak of others? Yes, the sweet – spirited French lady, **Madam Guyon** cannot be easily forgotten. This is a woman that lay long between **prison** walls. Like some caged birds that sing the sweeter for their confinement, the music of her soul has gone out far beyond the dungeon walls and scattered the desolation of many weak hearts

Let God isolate us for good relationship with him. If we neglect it, we not only rob ourselves, but others too, of blessing, since when we are blessed we are able to pass on blessing to others.

Is your loneliness as a result of death of spouse at old age? Don't be frustrated, the situation can knit you closer to God even than before. Let's hear what our great preacher **George Mueller** said of himself.

 "For sixty-two years and five months I had a beloved wife, and now, in my ninety-second year I am left alone. But I turn to the ever-present Jesus, as I walk up and down in my

room, and say, "Lord Jesus, I am alone, and yet not alone; you are with me, you are my friend"

At 92 years of age, George Mueller felt bad when he lost his dear wife, who he married for 65 years and 5 months! It was as if he was saying, 'O Lord, why do you do this to me? I am alone, my lovely jewel is gone. Who will cook and put delicious food on my table? Who can be so close to me like my wife, If not you Jesus'?

We must not allow fear find place in our lives as a result of loneliness. Chase spirit of fear out of your life by fire. Be filled with Spirit of God. You are a man/woman of war in the like of our creator. You must conquer, and not be conquered. You must excel to declare the glory of God.

To achieve this, you must declare loneliness and fear null and void in your life. You must pray fire prayer and belief in it.

Now let's pray.

PRAYER POINTS

I AM NOT ALONE JESUS IS WITH ME

1. O Lord, release me from every manner of bondage, in the name of Jesus

2. O Lord, give me what I desire to move me forward, in the name of Jesus

3. Spirit of loneliness in my life die, in the name of Jesus

4. Dark emotions in my life, expire and quit my life, in the name of Jesus

5. The sun shall not smite me by day, in the name of Jesus

6. The moon shall not smite me by night, in the name of Jesus

7. Spirit to care for and love my neighbor be my portion, in the name of Jesus

8. I shall discover myself by the power of the living God, in the name of Jesus

9. Every iron gate that captivates me, break to pieces in the name of Jesus

10. My God shall settle my case today in the name of Jesus

11. I shall not stumble, my enemies shall stumble in the name of Jesus

12. My destiny is settled in heaven for good, in the name of Jesus

13. I dash to pieces spirit of fear in the name of Jesus

14. O Lord, heal me of my wounds in the name of Jesus

15. Lord Jesus, terminate sickness in my life, in the name of Jesus

16. No fire shall burn me in the name of Jesus

17. My home shall not scatter in the name of Jesus

18. My spirit, come out of my father's house in the name of Jesus

19. My virtues in the warehouse of darkness, I recover you by fire in the name of Jesus

20. Spiritual handcuff in my hands break into pieces in the name of Jesus

21. Spiritual handcuff in my legs, break into pieces in the name of Jesus

22. My head shall not be exchanged for evil in the name of Jesus

23. Arrow of fear fired against me backfire in the name of Jesus

24. Power that kills fear, my life is open, enter, kill spirit of fear in my life, in the name of Jesus

25. Every dark covenant covering my glory, break, in the name of Jesus

26. Any covenant with family idols, I break you, in the name of Jesus

27. I destroy the grip of poverty in my life in the name of Jesus

28. I destroy pillar of delay, I rest upon, in the name of Jesus

29. Every power standing between me and my miracle, die in the name of Jesus
30. Power of hardship in my life, die, in the name of Jesus

31. My rod of success, swallow rod of failure assign against me in the name of Jesus

32. I shall not labour in vain, in the name of Jesus

33. Every network of witchcraft working against me scatter, in the name of Jesus

34. Hammer of God, break the backbone of poverty in my life in the name of Jesus

35. I recover, what spirit robbers stole from me in the name of Jesus

CHAPTER THREE
PROPHECY FOR CHAMPIONS

A car engine determines the speed of the car. If the engine is weak the car's speed will be low, but if it is new and powerful it will speed very well. This is how a man is in real life. The spiritual engine in you determines your prayer life. The level of your spirituality determines how far you can go. In the spirit the more you discover yourself, better for you to deal with giants that stir at you and say "I shall not let you go" "You are my victim".

As a champion in Christ, you need to pray and prophesy good things into your life, and declare, "I am not alone". Arise and pray with violent voice of a champion. Prophesy and paralyze activities of the wicked, distort their plans, scatter their moves against you. Render them useless, powerless and hopeless.

To achieve this, let prayer be your food. Let prophecies of liberty fill your mouth. Silence every power of darkness covering your destiny. It is you that will say no.

It is time to prophesy against loneliness, fear and defeat. Hence, prophesy into your life victory, surplus, progress, prosperity and spirituality as follows.

1. By word of prophecy, I am not alone; I am covered with blood of Jesus.

2. By word of prophecy, I am not alone; my sins are forgiven by Jesus Christ of Nazareth.

3. By word of prophecy, my God shall wash my iniquity and cleanse me from sin in the name of Jesus

4. By word of prophecy, though my sins are like scarlet they shall be as white as snow in the name of Jesus.

5. By word of prophecy, though my sins are red as crimson they shall be like wool, in the name of Jesus.

6. By word of prophecy, my Lord shall have mercy upon me, in the name of Jesus.

7. By word of prophecy, I call upon the Lord; he answers me, in the name of Jesus.

8. By word of prophecy, I call upon the Lord; he has compassion for me, in the name of Jesus.

9. By word of prophecy, my God shall turn his ear to my prayer, in the name of Jesus.

10. By word of prophecy, I am not alone, no temptation shall overcome me, in the name of Jesus.

11. By word of prophecy, I am precious in the eyes of God in the name of Jesus.

12. By word of prophecy, I shall be treated well wherever I go, in the name of Jesus.

13. By word of prophecy, days of fear are gone; my Lord is with me, in the name of Jesus.

14. By word of prophecy, I am not alone the eyes of the Lord is upon me, to guide and protect me in the name of Jesus.

15. By word of prophecy, I am not alone; the light of the Lord shall shine upon me in the name of Jesus.

16. By word of prophecy, my foundation is healed with blood of Jesus

17. By word of prophecy, I shall not walk in the counsel of the wicked, in the name of Jesus

18. By word of prophecy, I am not alone, I am with One mighty in battle

19. By word of prophecy, I am not alone, I shall not fail or fall in the name of Jesus

20. By word of prophecy, I am not alone, my God shall keep my lamp burning, in the name of Jesus.

21. By word of prophecy, I am not alone, Lord Jesus is with me, he shall open my soul to Holy Spirit in the name of Jesus

22. By word of prophecy, I am not alone, the Lord is the source of my mercy in the name of Jesus

23. By word of prophecy, I am not alone, my God shall hear my cry for mercy, in the name of Jesus

24. By word of prophecy, I and my household will trust in the Lord with all our hearts in the name of Jesus

25. By word of prophecy, I am not alone, my Lord shall keep my foot from evil in the name of Jesus

26. By word of prophecy, I am not alone, the Lord's command is a lamp for my greatness, his teaching a lamp of wisdom in the name of Jesus

27. By word of prophecy, I am not alone, my God equips me with weapons of war in the name of Jesus

28. By word of prophecy, I am not alone, no weapon fashioned against me shall prosper in the name of Jesus

29. By word of prophecy, I am not alone, my hands shall not forget its skill in the name of Jesus

30. By word of prophecy, I am not alone, my God shall train my hands for war, my fingers for battle in the name of Jesus

31. By word of prophecy, the banner of the Lord is upon me, in the name of Jesus.

32. By word of prophecy, I am not alone, I am strong in the Lord, in the name of Jesus

33. By word of prophecy, I am not alone, angels of the Lord shall ascend and descend for my sake, in the name of Jesus

34. By word prophecy, I receive royal power over all manner of situations in the name of Jesus.

35. By word prophecy, I am not alone, whoever touches me, touches the apple of God's eyes, and shall fail, in the name of Jesus

36. By word of prophecy, every obstacle and barriers fashion against me shall scatter in the name of Jesus

37. By word of prophecy, every cloud of darkness around me shall scatter and disappear in the name of Jesus

38. By word of prophecy, every chain of darkness fashion against me shall break to pieces in the name Jesus

39. By word of prophecy, I am not alone, every serpentine spirit pursuing me shall die in the name of Jesus

40. By word of prophecy, I am not alone; every witchcraft power assign to kill me shall die in the name of Jesus.

41. By word of prophecy, I am not alone; every plantation assign against me shall wither and die to the root, in the name of Jesus.

42. By word of prophecy, I am not alone; every curse pronounced against me shall back fire to sender, in the name of Jesus.

43. By word of prophecy, every covenant with dark power shall break, in the name of Jesus

44. By word of prophecy, I am not alone, every warfare against me shall scatter in the name of Jesus

45. By word of prophecy, I am not alone; every false witness that rises against me shall scatter, in the name of Jesus.

46. By word of prophecy, I am not alone, every injustice against me shall scatter, in the name of Jesus

47. By word of prophecy, I am not alone, every rebellion against me shall scatter, in the name of Jesus

48. By word of prophecy, I am not alone, strange arrows fired against me shall back fire and consume the sender, in the name of Jesus

49. By word of prophecy, I am not alone, arrow of death fired against me shall back fire and consume the sender in the name of Jesus

50. By word of prophecy, I am not alone, every arrow of poverty fired against me shall backfire and consume the sender, in the name of Jesus

51. By word of prophecy, I am not alone, arrow of sickness and disease fired against me shall back fire by fire in the name of Jesus

52. By word of prophecy, I am not alone; arrow of infirmity fired against me shall back fire by fire in the name of Jesus.

53. By word of prophecy, I am not alone, every arrow of nakedness fired against me shall go back and consume the sender, in the name of Jesus.

54. By word of prophecy, I am not alone, my God shall make me master over sorrow, in the name of Jesus

55. By word of prophecy, I am not alone, my God shall feed me with heavenly manna in the name of Jesus

56. By word of prophecy, I am not alone, my God shall heap calamities upon my enemies, in the name of Jesus

57. By word of prophecy, I am not alone, my God shall sharpen flashing sword against my adversaries in the name of Jesus.

58. By word of prophecy, I am not alone, my groans are over, in the name of Jesus

59. By word of prophecy, I am not alone, my God shall deliver me from the hands of the enemies in the name of Jesus

60. By word of prophecy, I am not alone; my eyes shall see visions, in the name of Jesus.

61. By word of prophecy, I am not alone, my burden is lifted; my yoke is broken in the name of Jesus.

62. By word of prophecy, I am not alone, my God shall turn insults of mockers back on their heads, in the name of Jesus

63. By word of prophecy, my enemies are clothed in shame, their tents are no more in the name of Jesus.

64. By word of prophecy, my God shall break the hands, evildoers stretch against me in the name of Jesus.

65. By word of prophecy, I am not alone, my God shall watch over my ways in the name of Jesus.

66. By word of prophecy, I am not alone, enemies of my soul shall turn back in sudden disgrace in the name of Jesus

67. By word of prophecy, I am not alone, the enemies of my soul are struck in the jaw, and their teeth are broken in the name of Jesus.

68. By word of prophecy, I am not alone, my God shall preserve seed of greatness in me in the name of Jesus.

69. By word of prophecy, I am not alone, my God rains fiery coals and burning sulfur upon my foes in the name of Jesus.

70. By word of prophecy, I am not alone, my God shall padlock the mouths of people that speak evil against me, in the name of Jesus

71. By word of prophecy, I am not alone, my God shall rescue me from the wicked by his sword in the name of Jesus.

72. By word of prophecy, I am not alone, my God shot arrow and scatter my enemies in the name of Jesus

73. By word of prophecy, I am not alone, my God is mighty behind me, he shall not turn me over to enemies, in the name of Jesus

74. By word of prophecy, I am not alone, my God shall set me free from dark traps in the name of Jesus

75. By word of prophecy, the Lord is my stronghold in time of trouble in the name of Jesus.

76. By word of prophecy, I am not alone, my God shall deliver me from death and my feet from stumbling in the name of Jesus

77. By word of prophecy, I am not alone, with his strong arm my enemies shall scatter in the name of Jesus.

78. By word of prophecy, I am not alone, my God shall send forth lightening and scatter my enemies in the name of Jesus

79. By word of prophecy, arrows of enemies shall not locate me in the name of Jesus

80. By word of prophecy, dark lions after me shall die, in the name of Jesus

81. By word of prophecy, blood suckers assigned to suck my blood, shall suck their own blood and die in the name of Jesus.

82. By word of prophecy, power of lust upon me shall die, in the name of Jesus

83. By word of prophecy, I break myself loose from dark covenants in the name of Jesus

84. By word of prophecy, I am not alone, bitterness in my soul shall die, in the name of Jesus

85. By word of prophecy, the pillars enemies rest on shall break to pieces by fire in the name of Jesus

86. By word of prophecy, every power after me shall paralyze in the name of Jesus

87. By word of prophecy, I am not alone, every violence directed at me shall scatter in the name of Jesus

88. By word of prophecy, I am not alone, troubles of the enemies shall coil round their necks in the name of Jesus

89. By word of prophecy, I am not alone, the violence of the wicked shall come upon them, in the name of Jesus

90. By word of prophecy, what I gather, enemies shall not scatter it, in the name of Jesus

91. By word of prophecy, graves of death fashioned against me shall scatter, in the name of Jesus.

92. By word of prophecy, foundations of enemies, shall shake and scatter, in the name of Jesus

93. By word of prophecy, I am not alone, evil plots and wicked schemes of the enemy shall not hold in the name of Jesus

94. By word of prophecy, I am not alone, enemies shall not triumph over me, in the name of Jesus

95. By word of prophecy, I am not alone, even though war break out against me, I will be confident in the name of Jesus

96. By word of prophecy, I am not alone, angels of the Lord shall drive enemies far away, in the name of Jesus

97. By word of prophecy, foot of the proud shall not come near me, in the name of Jesus

98. By word of prophecy, I am not alone, the Lord shall deliver me of trouble in the name of Jesus.

99. By word of prophecy, I am not alone, I shall not sit in darkness, in the name of Jesus

100. By word of prophecy, I am not alone, through Him; I push back enemies in defeat in the name of Jesus.

101. By word of prophecy, I am not alone, my eyes shall look in triumph on my foes, in the name of Jesus

102. By word of prophecy, I am not alone, fear and trembling are gone in my life, in the name of Jesus

103. By word of prophecy, I am not alone, tempest and storm against me shall scatter, in the name of Jesus

104. By word of prophecy, I am not alone, all that press attack against me shall scatter in the name of Jesus

105. By word of prophecy, I am not alone, enemies shall become like refuge on the ground, in the name of Jesus

106. By word of prophecy, tents of the wicked shall catch fire and roast to ashes in the name of Jesus

107. By word of prophecy, I am not alone, evildoers around me shall scatter, in the name of Jesus

108. By word of prophecy, I am not alone, my eye shall see the defeat of my adversaries in the name of Jesus

109. By word of prophecy, I am not alone, the boast of the enemy shall be silenced, in the name of Jesus

110. By word of prophecy, I am not alone, all manner of mountain shall melt before me in the name of Jesus

111. By word of prophecy, I will have nothing to do with evil, in the name of Jesus

112. By word of prophecy, I am not alone, all deep darkness that settles around me shall scatter, in the name of Jesus

113. By word of prophecy, enemies of my soul shall eat ashes as food, in the name of Jesus.

114. By word of prophecy, enemies of my soul shall be like desert owl, in the name of Jesus

115. By word of prophecy, enemies of my soul shall reduce to skin and bones, in the name of Jesus

116. By word of prophecy, enemies of my soul shall mingle their drinks with tears in the name of Jesus

117. By word of prophecy, the day of my enemies shall be like evening shadow that fades away quick in the name of Jesus.

118. By word of prophecy, my children shall live in my presence, I shall not bury one, in the name of Jesus

119. By word of prophecy, the days of stubborn pursuers are cut short, in the name of Jesus

120. By word of prophecy, my dread shall arrest enemies of my soul, in the name of Jesus

121. By word of prophecy, I shall not wonder away in life, in the name of Jesus

122. By hand of prophecy, I will rule in the midst of enemies in the name of Jesus

123. By word of prophecy, enemies shall break their teeth and waste away, in the name of Jesus

124. By word of prophecy, I am not alone, even in darkness, light shall shine upon me, in the name of Jesus

125. By word of prophecy, plans of the enemies against me shall scatter in the name of Jesus

126. By word of prophecy, when I lie down I will not be afraid, in the name of Jesus

127. By word of prophecy, sudden disaster shall not swallow me, in the name of Jesus

128. By word of prophecy, I shall not walk in crooked paths or in dark ways, in the name of Jesus

129. By word of prophecy, storm shall sweep the wicked away, in the name of Jesus

130. By word of prophecy, anger of the Lord shall fall upon the wicked, in the name of Jesus

131. By word of prophecy, whosoever dig pit for me, shall fall into it, in the name of Jesus

132. By word of prophecy, every enemy after my soul shall fall by the sword, in the name of Jesus

133. By word of prophecy, devourers assign against me shall devour themselves, in the name of Jesus

134. By word of prophecy, I am not alone, the ungodly shall bow before me in the name of Jesus

135. By word of prophecy, I am not alone, my God shall raise siege over my trouble waters, in the name of Jesus

136. By word of prophecy, the rod of God shall strike enemies of my soul to death, in the name of Jesus

137. By word of prophecy, looters assign against me in the spirit shall die, in the name of Jesus.

138. By word of prophecy, those who wage war against me shall be wasted, in the name of Jesus

139. By word of prophecy, I am not alone, my God shall turn rough places in my life to smooth path, in the name Jesus

140. By word of prophecy, I am not alone, when I pass through the river it will not sweep over me, because the Lord is with me

141. By word of prophecy, I am not alone, when I pass through the fire, it will not burn me, because the Lord is with me.

142. By word of prophecy, my God is with me, He shall do a new thing in my life, in the name of Jesus

143. By word of prophecy, tyranny against me shall die, in the name of Jesus

144. By word of prophecy, I shall live above bad news, in the name of Jesus

145. By word of prophecy, enemies of my soul shall crawl in disgrace in the name of Jesus

146. By word of prophecy, I am not alone, my God is with me, he that watches over Israel shall not slumber

147. By word of prophecy, I am not alone, my God shall keep me from deceitful ways, in the name of Jesus

148. By word of prophecy, I will soar on wings like eagles, in the name of Jesus.

149. By word of prophecy, my star shall rise and shine, in the name of Jesus

150. By word of prophecy, I am for the Lord, he engraves me on the palm of his hands in the name of Jesus.

151. By word of prophecy, those assigned to depose me shall be deposed, in the name of Jesus

152. By word prophecy, my ways shall be steadfast in obeying the Lord's decrees, in the name of Jesus

153. By word of prophecy, my God shall provide water for my thirst, and food when I am hungry, in the name of Jesus

154. By word of prophecy, those who mock me shall bow before me, in the name of Jesus

155. By the word prophecy, every manner of grief in my life shall disappear in the name of Jesus

156. By word of prophecy, my God shall make helpers scramble to help me in the name of Jesus

157. By word of prophecy, my God shall reveal himself to me in visions and speak to me in dreams, in the name of Jesus

158. By word of prophecy, I pronounce weakness into the life of enemy of my soul, in the name of Jesus

159. By word of prophecy, the anger of the Lord, shall burn against my enemies, in the name of Jesus

160. By word of prophecy, the light of my star shall shine in the name of Jesus

161. By word of prophecy, I am not alone, my Lord shall deliver my soul from powers of untimely death in the name of Jesus

162. By word of prophecy, I am not alone, my eyes are delivered from tears of disgrace and sorrow, in the name of Jesus

163. By word of prophecy, my legs shall not stumble in the name of Jesus

164. By word of prophecy, I am not alone, my God shall set me free, in the name of Jesus

165. By word of prophecy, my God shall reach down his hand to deliver me , in the name of Jesus

166. By word of prophecy, I am not alone, my God shall deliver me and rescue me from the hands of enemies, in the name of Jesus

167. By word of prophecy, I am a giant, not a grasshopper before my enemies in the name of Jesus.

168. By word of prophecy, I am not alone, I shall not fail the test of time, in the name of Jesus

169. By word of prophecy, I shall meet right people at the right time in right places, in the name of Jesus

170. By word of prophecy, I am rescued from calamities, in the name of Jesus

171. By word of prophecy, I shall not see trouble or grief in the name of Jesus.

172. By word of prophecy, my God is with me, he is my strength, my rock, my fortress and my deliver in the name of Jesus

173. By word of prophecy, I am saved from enemies of my soul, in the name of Jesus

174. By word of prophecy, I am not alone, I shall advance against a troop and defeat it, in the name of Jesus

175. By word of prophecy, my God is mighty, he delivers me from attacks of people in the name of Jesus

176. By word of prophecy, I shall be the head and not the tail, in the name of Jesus

177. By word of prophecy, I shall arise and stand firm, in the name of Jesus

178. By word of prophecy, my God shall not hide his face from me, in the name of Jesus.

179. By word of prophecy, I am independent of the wicked, in the name of Jesus

180. By word of prophecy, my God shall not turn deaf ear to me, in the name of Jesus

181. By word of prophecy, I am not alone, I will never be shaken, in the name of Jesus

182. By word of prophecy, I am not alone, my Lord is with me, I shall be strong in the Lord in the name of Jesus

183. By word of prophecy, I am not alone, I shall not lack good thing in the name of Jesus

184. By word of prophecy, I am not alone, I shall not bow my head in grief, in the name of Jesus

185. By word of prophecy, I am victorious over my adversaries, in the name of Jesus

186. By word of prophecy, I am not alone, I make covenant of peace with my Lord

187. By word of prophecy, I am not alone, I take refuge in the shadows of his wings until disaster passed in the name of Jesus

188. By word of prophecy, I shall not be fed with bread of tears in the name of Jesus

189. By word of prophecy, I devote my life and household to God, in the name of Jesus

190. By word of prophecy, my name shall not miss in the good register of God in the name of Jesus

191. By word of prophecy, I am loaded with strength, in the name of Jesus

192. By word of prophecy, the covenant of the Lord for me shall never fail, in the name of Jesus

193. By word of prophecy, I am save from fowler's snare in the name of Jesus

194. By word of prophecy, am save from deadly pestilence in the name of Jesus

195. By word of prophecy, I shall not fear terror of night in the name of Jesus

196. By word of prophecy, I shall not fear arrow that flies by day in the name of Jesus

197. By word of prophecy, I shall not fear pestilence that stalks in darkness in the name of Jesus

198. By word of prophecy, I shall not fear plagues that destroy by mid-day in the name of Jesus

199. By word of prophecy, I am not alone, a thousand may fall around me but it shall not come near me, in the name of Jesus

200. By word of prophecy, I am not alone, no disaster shall come near me in the name of Jesus

201. By word of prophecy, I am not alone, my God shall command his angels to guard me in all ways, in the name of Jesus

202. By word of prophecy, I am not alone, angels of God shall lift me up, I shall not strike my foot against a stone in the name of Jesus

203. By word of prophecy, I shall enjoy long life in the land of the living, in the name of Jesus

204. By word of prophecy, I shall dwell in the chamber of God, in the name of Jesus

205. By word of prophecy, I shall be outstanding among men, in the name of Jesus

206. By word of prophecy, I shall not fear what others fear because the Lord is with me in the name of Jesus

207. By word of prophecy, I will rule over oppressors, in the name of Jesus

208. By word of prophecy, I am not alone, my God shall keep me as the apple of his eye, in the name of Jesus

209. By word of prophecy, I am not alone, helpers shall not reject or forsake me, in the name of Jesus

210. By word of prophecy, I am not alone, I shall not be cast away in the name of Jesus

211. By word of prophecy, I am not alone, my God shall protect me from powers that rise up against me, in the name of Jesus.

212. By word of prophecy, my God shall deliver me from all evil, in the name of Jesus

213. By word of prophecy, my God shall save me from blood thirsty men, in the name of Jesus

214. By word of prophecy, my God shall lead me to the rock that is higher than me, in the name of Jesus

215. By word of prophecy, my God shall help and save me with his right hand, in the name of Jesus

216. By word of prophecy, every battle against me shall bow, in name of Jesus

217. By word of prophecy, the Lord is my rock and my salvation in the name of Jesus.

218. By word of prophecy, my God shall still the roar of wicked sea against me, in the name of Jesus

219. By word of prophecy, my prayer is accepted by fire in the name of Jesus

220. By word of prophecy, those who hope on lesser gods against me shall meet double failure, in the name of Jesus

221. By word of prophecy, I live above pit of hell, in the name of Jesus

222. By word of prophecy, my God is with me, I shall not retreat in disgrace in the name of Jesus

223. By word of prophecy, I am not alone, the foot print of the Lord is in my house in the name of disgrace

224. By word of prophecy, I am not alone, my God shall guide me to the point, I shall not be afraid, in the name of Jesus

225. By word of prophecy, I serve the God who maintains the rights of the poor and the oppressed, in the name of Jesus

226. By word of prophecy, I am not alone, I serve the God who delivers the weak and needy from the wicked.

227. By word of prophecy, darkness shall not take over my foundation in the name of Jesus

228. By word of prophecy, my crown shall not be defiled, in the name of Jesus

229. By word of prophecy, I am not alone, I shall be like mount Zion that cannot be shaken, in the name of Jesus

230. By word of prophecy, I am not alone, as the mountain surround Jerusalem, so shall angels of God surround me in the name of Jesus

231. By word of prophecy, I shall not be on bed of pain and sorrow in the name of Jesus

232. By word of prophecy, my God shall heal my wound, by his stripes I am healed in the name of Jesus

233. By word of prophecy, my bones are healed and strong, in the name of Jesus

234. By word of prophecy, valley of death shall not consume me, in the name of Jesus

235. By word of prophecy, terror of death shall vanish in my life, in the name of Jesus

236. By word of prophecy, death shall consume every enemy of my soul in the name of Jesus

237. By word of prophecy, my grieved heart is healed, in the name of Jesus

238. By word of prophecy, my body shall not serve as food to birds of the air, in the name of Jesus

239. By word of prophecy, I will not die but live, in the name of Jesus

240. By word of prophecy, spirit of death after my life shall die in the name of Jesus

241. By word of prophecy, my father, the great physician shall bind my wounds in the name of Jesus

242. By word of prophecy, my faith shall be strengthened in the name of Jesus

243. By word of prophecy, my faith shall rise, soar and claim my inheritance, in the name of Jesus

244. By word of prophecy, the anointing of the Lord is upon me in the name of Jesus

245. By word of prophecy, I receive pot of holy oil from above to baptize my destiny in the name of Jesus

246. By word of prophecy, my God shall bestow glory on me and lift my head to greater height, in the name of Jesus

247. By word of prophecy, my God shall crown me with glory and honour in the name of Jesus

248. By word of prophecy, my God anoints my head with oil, my cup overflows in the name of Jesus

249. By word of prophecy, my lip is anointed with oil of grace, in the name of Jesus

250. By word of prophecy, I am anointed with oil of joy in the name of Jesus

251. By word of prophecy, my Lord shall open my understanding to see his fullness in the name of Jesus

252. By word of prophecy, my God gives me heart of wisdom in the name of Jesus

253. By word of prophecy, I am loaded with reservoir of wisdom in the name of Jesus

254. By word of prophecy, anointing of the Lord is upon me every yoke confronting me shall break in the name of Jesus

255. By word of prophecy, by his anointing, I am free in the name of Jesus

256. By word of prophecy, I shall excel by his anointing upon me, in the name of Jesus

257. By word of prophecy, by his anointing, I am free from trouble and disgrace, in the name of Jesus

258. By word of prophecy, I am favoured in the name of Jesus

259. By word of prophecy, I am honoured in the name of Jesus

260. By word of prophecy, my God shall give me undivided heart to serve him, in the name of Jesus

261. By word of prophecy, Lord's goodness shall flow in my house in the name of Jesus.

262. By word of prophecy, I will be recorded among those who acknowledge God in the name of Jesus

263. By word of prophecy, my God shall satisfy me with unfailing love, in the name of Jesus

264. By word of prophecy, my Lord shall remember his love and faithfulness upon me, in the name of Jesus

265. By word of prophecy, I shall be remembered by friends and helpers, in the name of Jesus

266. By word of prophecy, the Lord's face shall shine upon me, for good, in the name of Jesus

267. By word of prophecy, the Lord is my redeemer and helper, in the name of Jesus

268. By word of prophecy, my God is an ever-present help in time of trouble, in the name of Jesus

269. By word of prophecy, people shall think kindness to me in the name of Jesus

270. By word of prophecy, from the rising of the sun, till it sets, I will be blessed, in the name of Jesus

271. By word of prophecy, I am not alone, my God is my help and shield in the name of Jesus

272. By word of prophecy, I shall draw from limitless purse of God, in the name of Jesus

273. By word of prophecy, I shall not experience money difficulty in the name Jesus

274. By word of prophecy, I am not alone, my God is my purse-bearer, therefore I shall not want, in the name of Jesus

275. By word of prophecy, I am not alone, I shall experience comfort from all corners of the world, in the name of Jesus

276. By word of prophecy, I shall be fruitful and multiply in wealth in the name of Jesus

277. By word of prophecy, my name shall be great and I shall be blessed in the name of Jesus
278. By word of prophecy, my God shall reward me handsomely in the name of Jesus

279. By word of prophecy, my home is full of silver and gold in the name of Jesus

280. By word of prophecy, my virtues in dark treasures shall be surrendered to me in the name of Jesus

281. By word of prophecy, I shall lend to many nations and borrow from none, in the name of Jesus

282. By word of prophecy, I shall lick honey from the rock in the name of Jesus

283. By word of prophecy, power of slave master upon me is broken, in the name of Jesus

284. By word of prophecy, the day of my birth is blessed in the name of Jesus

285. By word of prophecy, my dry seasons are over, in the name of Jesus

286. By word of prophecy, those who gather around me shall be a blessing to me in the name of Jesus

287. By word of prophecy, the blessing of the Lord is upon me, in the name of Jesus

288. By word of prophecy, I am well-watered plant in the name of Jesus

289. By word of prophecy, my God placed crown of pure gold on my head.

290. By word of prophecy, His rod and staff comfort me in the name of Jesus

291. By word of prophecy, my God pour fine oil of greatness upon me in the name of Jesus

292. By word of prophecy, I am not alone, I shall flourish like palm tree in the name of Jesus

293. By word of prophecy, my God shall satisfy my desires with good things, in the name of Jesus

294. By word of prophecy, my youth is renewed like eagles in the name of Jesus

295. By word of prophecy, my God shall perform miracles in my life, in the name of Jesus

296. By word of prophecy, hunger and thirst are gone forever in my life, in the name of Jesus

297. By word of prophecy, unfertile ground in my life shall become flowing springs of wealth, in the name of Jesus

298. By word of prophecy, I am not alone, streams shall flow in my desert in the name of Jesus

299. By word of prophecy, I am not alone, my God shall not delay to bless me in the name of Jesus

300. By word of prophecy, my destiny is open to gate of blessing in the name of Jesus

301. By word of prophecy, I am like olive tree that flourishes in the house of God

302. By word of prophecy, I receive heritage of the Lord in the name of Jesus

303. By word of prophecy, I am not alone, my God shall take me to palace of abundance in the name of Jesus

304. By word of prophecy, my land shall yield good harvest, my handwork shall not fail me, in the name of Jesus

305. By word of prophecy, strangers shall not plunder the fruit of my labour, in the name of Jesus

306. By word of prophecy, enemy may curse, but my God shall bless me in the name of Jesus

307. By word of prophecy, wealth and riches shall be found in my house, in the name of Jesus

308. By word of prophecy, I am not alone, my God lifted me from dung hill and seats me with princes and princesses in the name of Jesus

309. By word of prophecy, I will eat the fruit of my labour in Jesus name

310. By word of prophecy, blessing and prosperity are mine, in the name of Jesus

311. By word of prophecy, the hardship I endured shall be rewarded bountifully in the name of Jesus.
312. By word of prophecy, my foundation shall flourish in the name of Jesus

313. By word of prophecy, there is no end to my treasures in the name of Jesus

314. By word of prophecy, my God shall give me key of success, in the name of Jesus

315. By word of prophecy, wilderness is over in my life in the name of Jesus

316. By word of prophecy, I am placed in comfort zone, in the name of Jesus

317. By word of prophecy, shouts of joy shall sound loud in my house, in the name of Jesus

318. By word of prophecy, my heart is full of joy, in the name of Jesus

319. By word of prophecy, I shall serve my God with all my heart and rejoice, in the name of Jesus

320. By word of prophecy, I will be glad and rejoice in him, in the name of Jesus

321. By word of prophecy, my heart rejoices in his salvation in the name of Jesus

322. By word of prophecy, wasting diseases and sickness shall die in the name of Jesus.

323. By word of prophecy, I am not alone, there shall be confusion between my enemies and idol priests in the name of Jesus

324. By word of prophecy, I am not alone, troublers of my Israel shall experience double failure in the name of Jesus

325. By word of prophecy, I am not alone, my God shall blast to pieces altar of darkness in the name of Jesus

326. By word of prophecy, I am not alone, my God shall shut up boasting powers against me in the name of Jesus

327. By word of prophecy, testimonies of enemies against me shall be nullified in the name of Jesus

328. By word of prophecy, I am not alone, enemies of my soul shall experience double defeat in the name of Jesus

329. By word of prophecy, I am not alone, my Lord shall render my enemies powerless in the name of Jesus

330. By word of prophecy, those that plan to naked me shall be naked in the name of Jesus

331. By word of prophecy, I am not alone, every giant walking side by side with me shall die in the name of Jesus

332. By word of prophecy, I am not alone, any agent of death assign to kill me shall die in the name of Jesus

333. By word of prophecy, I am not alone, evil hands struggling with my property shall wither in the name of Jesus

334. By word of prophecy, my soul under arrest is released in the name of Jesus

335. By word of prophecy, I am not alone, every oracle against me shall die in the name of Jesus

336. By word of prophecy, spirit of poverty pursuing me about shall die in the name of Jesus

337. By word of prophecy, witchcraft merchant after my finance shall fail in the name of Jesus

338. By word of prophecy, dark kingdom that rise against me shall fail in the name of Jesus

339. By word of prophecy, owner of evil load shall carry their loads in the name of Jesus.

340. By word of prophecy, I am plugged into the socket of the Holy Ghost in the name of Jesus.

I am not alone; neither shall I be enslaved to fear, poverty or sorrow. By these prophecies, I am free, from satanic bondage in the name of Jesus. My prayers are sealed in heaven and shall be so. Henceforth, mercy of God shall be with me day and night in the name of Jesus. Amen.

The grace of the Lord Jesus Christ, the love of God, and sweet fellowship of the Holy Spirit shall be with me now and forever more. Amen.

Surely, goodness and mercy shall follow me all the days of my life forever and ever Amen

Praise the Lord! Alleluia.
Thank you Jesus, Amen.

YOU HAVE BATTLES TO WIN
TRY THESE BOOKS
1. COMMAND THE DAY

Each day of the week is loaded with meanings and divine assurance. God did not create each day of the week for the fun of it. Blessings, success, gifts, resources, hopes, portfolios, duties, rights, prophecies, warnings and challenges, are loaded in each day.

Do you know the language, command or decree you can use to claim what belongs to you in each day of the week? Do you know in Christendom; Monday can be equated to one of the days of creation in Genesis chapter one? Do you know creation lasted for six days and God rested on the seventh day? What day of the week can Christian equate as the first day of the week, if we follow Christian calendar? What day can we call day seven?

This book shall give insight to these questions. It shall explain how you can command each day of the week according to creation in the book of Genesis chapter one.

Above all, you shall exercise your right and claim what is hidden in each day of the week.

Check for this in **COMMAND THE DAY**

2. PRAYER TO REMEMBER DREAMS

A lot of people are passing through this spiritual epidemic on a daily basis. Their dream life is epileptic, having no ability to remember all dreams they dream, or sometimes forget everything entirely. This is nothing but spiritual havoc you need to erase from your spiritual record.

The answer to every form of spiritual blackout caused by spiritual erasers is found in, **PRAYER TO REMEMBER DREAMS.**

3. 100% CONFESSSIONS AND PROPHECIES TO LOCATE HELPERS.

This is a wonderful book on confessions and prophecies to locate helpers and helpers to locate you. It is a prayer book loaded with over two thousand (2,000) prayer points.

The book unravels how to locate unknown helpers, prayers to arrest mind of helpers and prayers for manifestation after encounter with helpers.

4. ANOINTING FOR ELEVENTH HOUR HELP.

This book tells much of what to do at injury hour called eleventh hour. When you read and use this book as prescribed fear shall vanish in your life when pursuing a project, career or contract.

5. PRAYER TO LOCATE HELPERS.
Our divine helper is God. He created us to be together and be of help to one another. In the midst of no help we lost out, ending our journey in the wilderness.

There are keys assign to open right doors of life. You need right key to locate your helpers. Enough is enough; of suffering in silence.

With this book, you shall locate your helpers while your helpers shall locate you

6. FIRE FOR FIRE PRAYER BOOK
This prayer book is fast at answering spiritual problems. It is a bulldozer prayer book, full of prayers all through. It is highly recommended for night vigil. Testimonies are pouring in daily from users of this book across the world!

7. PRAYER FOR THE FRUIT OF THE WOMB
This prayer book is children magnet. By faith and believe in God Almighty, as soon as you use this

book open doors to child bearing shall be yours. Amen

8. PRAYER FOR PREGNANT WOMEN

This is a spiritual prayer book loaded with prayers of solution for pregnant women. As soon as you take in, the prayers you shall pray from day one of conception to the day of delivery are written in this book.

9. WARFARE IN THE OFFICE

It is high time you pray prayers of power must change hands in office. Use this book and liberate yourself from every form of office yoke.

10. MY MARRIAGE SHALL NOT BREAK

Marriage is corner piece of life, happiness and joy. You need to hold it tight and guide it from wicked intruders and destroyer of homes.

11. DICTIONARY OF DREAMS

This is a must book for every home. It gives accurate details to about **10,000 (Ten thousand) dreams and interpretations,** written in alphabetical order for quick reference and easy digestion. The book portrays spiritual revelations with sound prophetic guidelines. It is loaded with Biblical references and violent prayers.

Ask for yours today.

For Further Enquiries Contact
THE AUTHOR
EVANGELIST TELLA OLAYERI
P.O. Box 1872 Shomolu Lagos.
Tel: 08023583168

FROM AUTHOR'S DESK

Authors write for others to digest, gain and broaden intellects. Your comment is therefore needed to arouse others into Christ's bosom.

I therefore implore you to comment on this on this book.

God bless.

Thanks.

CPSIA information can be obtained
at www.ICGtesting.com
Printed in the USA
LVHW080614150420
653534LV00009B/700